"These finely crafted poems explore the rich diversity of life and do not shrink from the harsh realities of divorce, bewilderment, homelessness, or the stray dogs left behind. The poems are sometimes heartbreaking but also compassionate as they lean toward hope of rescue, of redemption. Pleimann writes of the harsh realities of life with a generous and open heart. He understands that words are like snakes we sleep with and handles them carefully."

—MICHAEL HOGAN
Author of *In the Time of the Jacarandas*

"John Pleimann is a magician of words that come alive on the page, just as does the child in 'Come Shivering to Collect,' who shows up at his door to collect, but instead ends up giving him a prized stone and an unforgettable poem. In his precision to invite the mysteries of words to reveal their hidden meanings, his readers are drawn into a mysterious world where every word is a spell in itself, a waking dream, 'a dark corner / where love and loathe are trying to couple.' Pleimann is not only an astonishing poet, but a memorable teacher who opens the curtains of the page to reveal unexpected truths."

—HOWARD SCHWARTZ
Author of *The Library of Dreams: New & Selected Poems 1965–2013*

"The poems in *Come Shivering to Collect* brilliantly display that 'within restraint lies great intensity,' as William Butler Yeats observed. The compression of each line in these poems as it unfolds, enfolds, and refolds the language tells us something that we have never heard before. The beauty of the execution is often so direct, often so simple, they can turn a simple child's game of 'you're it' into a revelation of aging, loss, and alienation. *Come Shivering to Collect* is poetry at its finest."

—WALTER BARGEN
First Poet Laureate of Missouri

"Pleimann confronts the difficulty, confronts the shock of the *unknown-brought-forth*, confronts the swervings and close-calls that equal each waking day, that equal a life in poem after brilliant poem. Readers often turn to philosophy for *truth*, but find it, as they will here, more often, more candidly, and more movingly in poetry."

—ERIC PANKEY
Professor of English, Heritage Chair in Writing,
George Mason University

Come Shivering to Collect

Come Shivering to Collect

Poems

John Pleimann

COME SHIVERING TO COLLECT
Poems

Copyright © 2021 John Pleimann. All rights reserved. Except for brief quotations in critical publications or reviews, no part of this book may be reproduced in any manner without prior written permission from the publisher. Write: Permissions, Slant Books P.O. Box 60295, Seattle, WA 98160.

Slant Books
P.O. Box 60295
Seattle, WA 98160

www.slantbooks.com

HARDCOVER ISBN: 978-1-63982-097-9
PAPERBACK ISBN: 978-1-63982-096-2
EBOOK ISBN: 978-1-63982-098-6

Cataloguing-in-Publication data:

Names: Pleimann, John.
Title: Come shivering to collect : poems / John Pleimann.
Description: Seattle, WA: Slant Books, 2021.
Identifiers: ISBN 978-1-63982-097-9 (hardcover) | ISBN 978-1-63982-096-2 (paperback) | ISBN 978-1-63982-098-6 (ebook)
Subjects: LCSH: American poetry — 21st century. | American poetry. | Poetry.
Classification: PS3566.L3 P545 2021 (paperback) | PS3566.L3 (ebook)

10/19/21

*For Amy, my pups Maxie, Welkin, Joco, and Rusty,
my family and friends.*

CONTENTS

I.
Syllabic | 3
Love Would Be Good | 4
Come Shivering to Collect | 6
Look Twice before Crossing | 8
Had Anyone Cared to Listen | 9
There | 10
The Name | 11
This | 12
It | 14
The Bay | 16
They Is | 18
This Way | 19
Taxonomy | 20
Plowman's Prayer | 21

II.
Stray | 25
Head On | 27
Still Moving | 29
AM | 31
At The Back of His Cage | 32
Dead People's Clothes: Care Instructions | 34
Hair of The Dog | 36
Water Bowl | 37
On | 38
Broken Man, Broken | 39

Room | 40
Lonely Only Once | 42
From Around Here | 44
Falsetto | 46
Stay Warm | 48
Rejoice | 49
In Your Fist | 50
Dead Deer Beside WIS 44 | 52
Will I Have? | 53
Heft and Threat | 54

III.

Brother, Can You? | 59
Who, You? | 61
Sending Anna Home | 62
Outside the Fact | 64
All Grown Up | 65
Diviner | 66
Her Song | 68

IV.

For the Walgreens Christmas Eve Crew | 71
Blue Time | 73
Be Quiet | 74
If You Had To | 76
Even the Dishes | 78
Below the Gospel Tent | 80
Believers | 82
Last Rites | 84
In Quiet Cafes | 85
Strewn | 87
Sweet Assassin | 89
Final Draft of A Note to Myself | 91

Acknowledgements | 93

I.

SYLLABIC

As if sound were sense enough,
my tongue today insisted *succulate*
a word. It was a mouth meaning,
juice of *succubus* and *succulent*
a word between, a word my tongue
lay down with in the dark.

I nippled it, rubbed it against *suckle,*
let it nurse me after my wife explained
with rhetorical precision the marriage
was gone. *Succulate* stayed moist.

Anymore, the words that speak for me,
are close but closed to reason, the nano-
syllabic, the ones only I can hear
as in *succulate* and its overtones:
you suck, you suck too late,
too late, sucker.

LOVE WOULD BE GOOD

Ben was a bad student.
I planned to tell him so,
to explain that his poem "How
to Urinate" was unworthy
of urinal graffiti.

I was six months divorced,
eleven months without
a woman's embrace, no one
to call if I awoke into
the dead eye of night. I
had no heart to be direct.

Five weeks straight I taught
my class the power of tone, irony,
connotation, how nothing
could be told straight because
nothing ever was what it seemed.

"Words are lies," I thundered
like a prophet, "even words
from the heart. You can spend
your life pushing words around
and find you were chasing
what you could only say
without them."

Those five weeks I found myself
spread around the house:
bruised pears in a splintered bowl,
the red zero on my answering machine,
dead flies caught between the screen
and window.

It was time to make tropes.
The book suggested *Love is.*
Love is like. I said,
"It's been overdone. What about
Loneliness is or Stupidity is like,"
but no one looked at me

except for Ben, who had never
looked away, Ben who had not read
the assigned chapter but read
my eyes and in his dreamy, drawn-
out voice said "Yeah, love
would be good," and in a voice
softer and dreamier than his,
I agreed, as if I had heard myself
from far away,

as if the bad student in me knew
it was time for the teacher to learn
an easy answer the hard way.

COME SHIVERING TO COLLECT

A child with a full moon face
stands at my front door.
He has come to collect for something
to which I must have agreed.
The lines of his open palm
branch toward me.

He cannot say what I owe,
as if to reveal would lose me,
and I am all he has left.
He looks at my address and weeps.

I reach for my wallet,
but his eyes confess he has
nothing to win, no goal,
no quota, no one to hold him
accountable.

He takes from inside his mouth
a smooth stone and puts it
in my palm, folds my fingers
and whispers to my fist.

The moon tonight hangs bruised
and full, streetlights
flicker on. This child,
come shivering to collect,
turns away in silence.

The stone grows cold and heavy
in my fist, my fist
which will not open,
even though I command it.

LOOK TWICE BEFORE CROSSING

There's never any blood when you call it road kill.
The words are styptic with a built-in laugh track
every bit as fake as the one on *I Love Lucy*.

When you call it road kill, it's only a furry patch
of asphalt, stone deaf to any bone or flesh broken
or ripped, stone deaf to any sound the creature made.

The accent is on road not kill, so your voice grinds
death into the earth, and you slip by with a steel-belted
hum that numbs your urge to stop and check for signs of life.

When you know what words can do, take them on the road.
Call your failing marriage road kill, your best friend's betrayal
road kill, your tearless grief at Mother's funeral road kill.

There's nothing words can't keep from you, no emptiness
around you words can't flesh out, nothing words can't clean
up when things spill out that other words can't contain.

HAD ANYONE CARED TO LISTEN

On my way back to bed,
I heard my father hum
to Mendelssohn or Brahms
in the dark living room.

He stopped when I passed by.
Ice cubes clinked,
and his cigarette's glow
grew more intense,
while the record spun on.

He was never in tune,
and had an odd counterpoint,
as if the music that played
was little more than prelude
to what he could have done
had anyone cared to listen.

It was as though
he had claimed
against the composer

"You have been trained
to arouse feeling,
but listen,

this is what it's like to feel
without form
or measure."

THERE

Words are everything else in the world.
—Wallace Stevens

Lost at sea,
dying of thirst,
he wants earth
more than water.
He wants to die
on solid ground.

A sliver of land,
thumbnail thick
at the horizon
will stop thirst
from sinking in.

He lays his finger
on what he sees
and says "There,"
as if the word will
carry him ashore,

as if his breath
were wind enough
to keep afloat
the hope on which
his finger sets sail.

THE NAME

Dead child, dead dog,
dead father, dead wife.
You pray their names
on fire each night.

You bless their days
and give them back.
How flesh the spirit,
how dry the dark.

Your breath comes in.
Your voice goes out.
You say so little,
you wait so far.

You sigh, you laugh.
You listen for each
new day, new night
to listen back, to reach

through distance fact
and word must keep
because to pray
is to believe

the name will speak.

THIS

Open any black box
salvaged from disaster
and you hear
"Oh, God, Oh, no,"
the sound of
everything right
gone wrong at once.

You hear the cry
of your soul cast up
to light still blinding
from birth,
your disbelief
that all goes on
without you.

It's the inconceivable
nosediving
through vital organs like
a miracle decommissioned
without apology.

It's the darkness
every black box
builds itself around,
which is the life
you never
make it out of,

the life you build
around
a black box
your voice
echoes inside
until you declare
"Oh, God, Oh, no,"

choked and low, heaven
yanked to earth in
guttural glory,

as if this was all
you meant, all
you had ever meant
and why had it taken
all this time to be heard
and pored over
for telltale signs

of great and heavenly
portent.

IT

"You're it," he yells.
The other kids
squeal and dart.

Someone giggles
behind a bush,
sees you coming
and disappears.
A boy runs by,
but your finger can't
quite reach
when he arcs his back
and slips past.

It's getting dark.
You circle in place
to find
the weakest kid
and make him
what you no longer
can stand to be.

Your mother calls,
"Time to come in."
Now, you're not it.
Mother's voice
is outside the game,
so the kid whose rump
you're about to tag
yells "Everybody's it,"
and you're free
to be you.

The game is over,
but the rules go on.
Birthdays pass like stars
turned off each morning.
And there you are 35,
45, 55, exceeding
all age limits.

Twilight falls fast.
Your mother isn't there
to call you home.
You're it, but no one
bothers to run.

THE BAY

Tonight, I free
the gulls,

clip the word "gulls"
of wings.

Gulls come alive
in sky so close

my body swoops
to wing-tipped water

and feeds in flight.
What have I missed?

How can I say "bird"
or "bay" and not get wet?

Words have tongues,
shadows underwater

rising hard,
falling silent

to the sediment
of said,

as if to say as dumb
as dirt is best

when fish not word
nibbles the lip.

THEY IS

—After Tobias Wolff's "Bullet in the Brain"

With a bullet midway through his brain
and on its way out, he's free to think,
free to remember Gilbert Jackson, who said
in seventh grade of playing shortstop,
"They is no better position."

He's free to forget he savored Gilbert's
error, free to regret he ever believed one
had to know the rules to break them, free
to confirm grammar has logic but no voice.

He's free to admit "They is" was not ignorance
but the story of a boy's life in a small town
where chain link fence curled from the backstop
post, where boys caught flyballs with two hands,
where bad grammar meant good friends.

He's free to see what lies beneath him is not
a symbol, a simile, a trope to open
in one of his urbane book reviews,
but simply the spreading pool of his own blood
into which he's free to collapse and think
"What don't need no grammar saves you."

THIS WAY

Each fork of a rattlesnake tongue
divines odor that says predator/prey,
this way home.

Fourteen point seven pounds
per square inch on a man's flesh
divine the god out there needs

the god within all the way
to troposphere, where divinity ends
and words fall like rain or manna.

The body is a word that crawls,
divining its death and turning
to tongues that say predator/prey,

this way home, where the heart is
or some such thing filled with blood
reaching down as you reach up.

TAXONOMY

—For Amy

The song I wrote about your hands
became the poem I wrote about your legs,
became the phone call I began,
became the letter I unsealed to revise

until a snowy egret rose
from the marsh and carried
my words through an aperture
into dusk.

I see much better in the dark. Shadows turn
inside out and there, a strand of your hair
on the hallway floor like some cursive letter
from a language that's trying to learn me.

One day your black hair went wild
across your eyes, and you smiled like a child
playing hide-and-seek. *Egretta thula* rises
unbidden to my lips.

I'm not sure if that's right, but before I can check,
the egret returns and settles out of sight,
the way all new words for love
begin in augury and divination.

PLOWMAN'S PRAYER

Let my words be simple, elemental,
able when their crop is taken,
to be plowed back under

into something richer, something
I could not imagine.
Let the beast that plods before me

comprehend a subtle shift of hand
and keep each row proportionate
as we follow angles of the sun.

Let me be a man turning words
back to life, to light not stellar
but diffuse, like moonlight spread

across some field I must cross
by foot, by dream, by shadow.

II.

STRAY

A stray dog leaped out of shadow
and somehow dodged my bumper
in Highway 90's morning traffic.

Panting hard, he jumped the median,
stayed close, went with the flow.
His odds grew ugly against five lanes
of rush hour rushing.

I watched him in my rear-view mirror
and leaned toward the median in prayer,
to keep him calm, to keep him still,
until an opening. There was no end
to the burst of brakelights, as scarlet
as an old scar torn open.

All the way to work, I leaned against
the door; something in me wanted out,
wanted to go back and jump beside him.

I leaned into every corner of the day
I could find: kept my office door closed,
let my voice-mail speak for me, ate
my lunch alone and then drove home.

There was blood but no dog. Maybe
he limped off to die beneath a bush, maybe
he limped off to heal beneath a bush, maybe
he is still flying through the air, maybe
he will never land.

The shadow from which he leaped
darkens each day, follows me home, and
the traffic inside stays backed up
for miles.

HEAD ON

When the horn beeped, I awoke.
From the upstairs window,
I saw my father slumped

against the steering wheel,
his forehead against his hands
gripping the wheel at 12:00.

He appeared dead, ill, pleading
like a priest defrocked.
The car's angle said he was drunk.

I should have gone to him, but there he was
in the dome light's pall, the door ajar as if
he wanted out but didn't dare move, darkness

spread around his car like a nightmare.
Ten years old, I understood things fall
some men cannot steer around.

Given the swerving and languid blinks,
how does a man make it home that drunk
without taking a life?

Does he make it home because he knows
from far away the porch light
has been turned on?

Does he make it home because when he turns off
the ignition, all engines stop, and the pings
of contracting metal speak softly?

Does he make it home because the child he was
rides in the seat beside him?
I stood too long at the windowsill believing

he was dead. I should have gone to him and said
"Father, come inside, you made it, we're home,"
but the dome light shone funereal,

and the headlights, the headlights
were still on, the high beams
somewhere out there swerving,

swerving, and then drifting, drifting
into another life coming fast,
head on.

STILL MOVING

As if the words Platonic and plate tectonic
drift over one another as they rise
from a blue background of atonement,
and you feel the dark earth shift
beneath your bare feet,
while some ideal form hangs
out there, always out there,
like a Siren of space and time
to say all guilt might erase
if you keep moving toward the door.

One thing wants to mean another,
to slip by that dark corner
where love and loathe are trying to couple.
You recall what could have been
only to look down and find yourself
two continents away, still moving,
and behind sits your note on the kitchen table.

Not even you recognize the handwriting,
or the voice behind your words.
Too much of what you think you know,
no, too much of what you think
sounds close, as in almost, and close
as in a door you, yourself, left open,
never clear if you were coming or going.

You sound like a stranger
mumbling to himself
on his way out or in, wherever
you are not.

AM

When your telephone rings at four in the morning,
there's no time to send postcards you promised,
no time to make up the time you cancelled:
someone you love is lost or dead.

When your telephone rings at four in the morning,
your bones condense, your blood thickens,
your lips part, the dark room
takes a big breath all around you.

When your telephone rings at four in the morning,
you stab for the receiver as though your loved one's hand
just slipped from the wrong side of a bridge over
a river running through you.

When your telephone rings at four in the morning,
you press the earpiece close and listen deep
to the split-second silence before some stranger asks
if you're who they think you are

and the quick, desperate breath when you say "Yes"
as if this time you mean it.

AT THE BACK OF HIS CAGE

You came for a puppy, but now you stand
by the big dog, alone in his cage, the dog
no one has lost, and no one will adopt.
You know he's put down within the week,
but you stand there as if teasing
a bad molar with your tongue.

His eyes have gone slack. He sits
at the back of his cage, trying
to forget his legs, his bark,
the fields of high grass.

Maybe you can buy them all back
if you stand there long enough.
Maybe there's a lot to redeem
if you stand there long enough.

Maybe the Sundays your mother waited
beside the telephone, melancholy,
maybe the Tuesdays your father thought
you might call and take him to lunch,
maybe the years your wife spent wondering
what she was doing wrong
are sitting inside that cage for you
to take them home. One eye on you,

one you can't see, he sits
outside his life.
The attendant flickers the light
to let you know your time is up.

Don't let them put him down, don't
make him sit through one more night
of yelps and cries from other dogs

who still want out. He is the dog
you came for, the dog you hoped
you would never find, the dog who lost
his legs to memory, to fields
he would never run again. A field

is opening inside of you,
and you could run free
if you just stood still
inside his life inside yours.

DEAD PEOPLE'S CLOTHES: CARE INSTRUCTIONS

Boots and shoes should be
the first to go; emptiness
stands in them all day and
never steps out.

Keep no clothes hanging
in the closet. Memories
try to fill them, a slight
breeze brings them
back to life.

Clean out the drawers.
Everything folded
is a gift you will
never receive.

Pack what's left into bags
and leave them
for charity to pick up
when you're gone.

Be ready for items
you somehow forget:
work gloves in the shed,
sunglasses in the glovebox,
an undershirt in the rag box,
a hat on a hook, cocked
at an odd angle,

a black sweater draped
over the back of a black chair
whose sleeves might rise
and lean against the desk
but only if you turn away
and let the spirit dress.

HAIR OF THE DOG

You raise your hand to smack her hard
when she bounds too soon into the house,
paws muddy from a backyard patch worn bare.
Your hand stops, hovering as if you're about
to witness or take an oath, your teeth tight
behind pressed lips.

Whatever she's going to learn about muddy paws
and rainy days or about thunder and lightning
in your voice will be lost on her, lost in you
if you inflict the pain you swear she deserves.

You stand there in your kitchen cursing God and beat
the air above her head to test how much you mean
to carry through. Why don't you take the towel,
wipe her paws, whisper "What a messy girl
you are," and then forgive yourself?

Here she is, cowering at your feet,
ears back, eyes set to close, and whatever
you were going to strike has slunk off
to a corner, fearing the shadow of your hand.

WATER BOWL

Six weeks on, I keep water
in my dead dog's bowl, something
to do with keeping her spirit close, something
to do with grief confronting a moat, something
to do with light her eyes closed over when
the doctor said "Hold her, keep her still,"
something each day to empty and fill.

ON

The day you stop for the dazed and bloody possum
is the one day you are late for work, late
for your big presentation, your terminal chance
to shine. It's the day something in you says
wear the white pinpoint Oxford, not the powder blue,
and if your heart is in it, stop for animals dazed
and bloody beside the road.

It's the day you're as crisp and brilliant as your shirt,
the day when what you have to say is Greenwich
mean-time calibrated, the day you're on, the day
not even you--least of all you--can quite believe
how well you come across. You stand there

with a California smile, your slideshow humming
like a private jet, bloody paw prints skittered
up your shirt, your audience rapt, not sure
where you begin and the last two possum tracks, one
each side of your throat, end.

BROKEN MAN, BROKEN

Broken man, broken, the short days of winter
shadow bellies of wounded beasts. Come spring,
butterflies die wing by wing in your chest.

Broken man, broken, the children
you never had call collect for imagined advice
and send their love from private schools

whose windows go dark when you look,
whose rooms fall to ash and embers
if you enter without knocking.

Broken man, broken, prophet, mendicant,
monk who cowls his head,
be careful if you pray what you need,

for the road beneath your tongue
walks its own way, and how are you
to travel far from what you know?

Broken man, broken, drum this ground
you have walked from birth to here, now,
this place, pumped with heat you hold

like an oath sworn with your palm
above a candle flame you bear
to a burn wound beyond healing

but not beyond this life whose love
is all the story you need tell and will,
so help me, God.

ROOM

You were lucky to find
a bigger home close
to where you lived,
but when it was time
to leave, something
welled up and stuck inside
you like a door
in wet weather.

Your two dogs lived
and died here,
your father's death
caused the telephone
in this bedroom to ring,
here's the hearth
where you kept a fire
and read winter hours,
this bathroom mirror
confirmed your presence
each morning,
this sunroom was a greenhouse
for your daydreams.

Weekend afternoons
you opened blinds
on all four sides
and let the house flood
with sun. That light
must stay behind.

You believe
you lived here,
but did you live
as deeply
as all the open doors
suggest?

What you held back
still lives here, has rights
to stay and will.

Before you lock the door
and leave the key, you check
one last time, running
room-to-room as if to catch
yourself in some intimate act.
You stand there breathing
hard, turning in circles
to witness the space
that lives inside.

Something is moving,
but you don't need
to check what it is.
You've moved away enough
to know the sound
of coat hangers rocking
in an empty closet.

LONELY ONLY ONCE

Tonight, it's walnut-crusted Mahi-Mahi,
risotto, Caesar salad, fresh baguette
with olive oil and oregano, 1992 Shiraz,
kiwi sorbet and, yes, two candles
on my table for a party of one.

All month, I waited for you to write,
all the month before for you to call.
Quiet days silt to silence, rooms lose
their memory when I enter.

Remember the woman below in Naples,
dining al fresco on her balcony, starched linen,
tapered candle, bone china, silverware
wrapped in a silk napkin? We said how sad
to have no one with whom to share, but then,
she held her crystal wine glass to the moon
and lowered to her lips a lover's kiss.

She comes to me tonight, singular
as I am, clouds crossing the moon
like a Carthusian monk slipping on
his cowl. Atonement is at-one-ment.
I never meant to be just one, but one is
what I am. I raise my wine glass and toast
all out there between us as if it were all
we might someday harvest.

Let me add because I must,
you have to be lonely only once
to know lonely's metallic breath, its filthy
fingernails under your skin, the dead arm
it drapes across your chest,
the neon *Vacancy* sign
pulsing in the rented room
your heart lies down in.

If you get this letter, just let me know,
please, just.

FROM AROUND HERE

There's nothing here he loves, but he loves
driving through these rusted
little towns where people mostly live
to work, and when they're out of work
they stay because it's home and "Home
Sweet Home" is how the afghan reads,
the one some guy pulls over himself,
watching *The Sands of Iwo Jima* at 2 a.m.
because tomorrow is on its way too soon
for him to forget he's no longer proud to be
Union Steel. Mom-and-pop stores

go under beside mom-and-pop franchise
operations and one mega-supercenter.
These towns are tinged in gray, primer
gray, a color that says maybe there's no need
for a top coat, maybe this is it.
They bring him to a place that feels
like home, even if he's glad it's not
and never will be. He drives through them
or stops to get gas and stands at the pump
watching what it costs to keep moving.

He drives past names, but never stops
to think why they make steel in Granite
City, why Pendleton doesn't leave him
warm and fuzzy, why Oakville is mostly pine.
He drives past trees whose names he swears
someday he's going to learn
because it's one way to make them stand still,
one way for him to stay, but he passes them
and they pass him when he looks back.

Maybe not people so much as place is what
he holds inside his heart. How else
to explain land that never lets go, land
his memory runs through before it gets to him,
land that fails to call him home.

Rows of corn flip by like pages in a book
without pagination, without characters
or plot, and there he is moving in shadow
fluttering across the corn stalks, waving
to himself in silhouette just to be sure
it's him moving to some other rusted town
where there is nothing he loves.

FALSETTO

It's pledge week again on PBS,
commercial-free, no-strings-attached TV
whose mission is to edify, enlarge, enrich,
and to periodically suggest you are one
freeloading son-of-a bitch.

You have held off this three-week siege
against your credit card, but PBS knows
what you deny: you like to get misty
and reminisce and sing falsetto
in your living room, alone.

In a phalanx of 60s nostalgia,
they've arranged one-hit bands
to take your heart in 4/4 time
and get you to pledge after Percy
Sledge hammers you hard.

If that can't move you, they have saved
one sweaty singer who looks like you,
receding hairline, puffy jowls,
whose voice is still in its 20s,
and when he howls two octaves up,

you try to hit what you hit back then,
but you try too hard and settle down,
humming and tapping your heels,
eyes closed, the audience on their feet
to let him know he still has it.

An operator is standing by to let you know
you still have it, but now it's time
to give it up. Her voice rises
when she hears the raspiness of yours.
She wants to know you and your name

as it appears on your credit card,
and when you're done surrendering
what she wants, she wants to know
if you could, please, confirm
the expiration date.

Oh-1, oh-4, oh-7 sounds like such
a lamentation to what was,
you ask if it's too late to pledge
one level higher, one level up,
one level more—you're not sure
how to say it, but you know it's more
than you knew was in you.

STAY WARM

I found the old coat you lost
but never tried to find, as if
an old coat were something else
you couldn't care less about.

At the bus stop, in the bleachers,
on the trail to Angel Mountain,
this coat held your heat
and never left you cold.

Did you ever stop to imagine it
bunched up in some alley, stuffed
in the trunk of some stranger's car,
flapping wildly from a dead branch?

Did you reconsider the hostess's smile
when she said, "Well, now. I guess
it just walked off without you"?

Were you comforted to recall
its missing buttons, loose lining,
torn collar, frayed sleeves
and other signs of life?

I found it spread-eagled beneath
Highway 32's rush-hour traffic.
People swerved at first, but those
behind caught on and drove
right over it.

REJOICE

When you heard
the flattened third,

you fell
so in love with pain

you held this note
like a baby bird

dead from its nest,
eyes closed,

head twisted to one side,
yellow beak agape

as if the note begins
but never ends,

and so the heart
must temper

birth inside death, death
inside birth, so open

and empty one returns
to the nest

like a flattened third
so blue you fly.

IN YOUR FIST

I.

One day something in you
        clicks
like tumblers in a lock

and rain that fell upon you,
        falls now far away
over land that swings

        open and closed
on the broken hinges
        in your fist.

II.

You will never
        have
children.

You will never
        love
yourself, but love

the idea of yourself
        in children
you will never have.

III.

The older you get,
        the closer to God
you become,

        so bless yourself
because redemption
        is for bottles,

and much of you remains
        to be filled
without the least bit
        of irony.

DEAD DEER BESIDE WIS 42

A two-lane blood stain trails
to the shoulder like a secret
you cannot keep.

In rigor mortis, her legs splay
from a belly so white and open
she arcs one more time

into a night whose stars
burn beneath your skin
like headlights that froze

her last second, that bridge
you better cross, splayed
and tender as you are,

becoming more a secret
you cannot keep, cannot tell,
cannot swerve around.

You are not a simile struck blind.
You're a two-lane blood stain.

WILL I HAVE?

Will I have washed the air
of worry and slapped
the moon to shine me
all the way through?

Will I have pressed my love
into the hands of a lover
who promised in song
my death by song?

Will I have wrapped my arms
around myself as if to feel
how common and frail
one must be for love to open,

for love to open
all the windows so birds
are states of mind,

and questions
no longer pound
like manifestos?

HEFT AND THREAT

—First Unitarian Church

I.

I come early to sit alone
before voices burr the hush
and shelve my breath.

In stained glass light,
I open to the days
after I die, crossing now

like shadows on my lungs.
Sunray dust motes dance
to music unmaking.

I fold my hands
and hold me to myself
as if a friend

for whom I matter,
and so my heart its own
atonement.

II.

I come early to catch me
quiet and cornered
that my flesh bear its heft

and threat and I feel
my feet grounds for belief,
my arches an apse

in which to pray.

III.

I come early to sit quiet
in a body whose heart
seems weary and aloof

as if it calls me
from a meadow everywhere
at once that all the world might hear
how thin and human this voice
I press too hard to convey
the heaven of earth.

All day, low clouds
chant Gregorian.

III.

BROTHER, CAN YOU?

—Outside Walgreens

You try to believe he works here
and the ashtray sand falling
through his fingers
is routine maintenance, but
believing is not seeing.

He's sifting for cigarette butts
to hold off hunger, to draw heat
into his chest; it's single-digit cold
and falling.

You try to believe your credit cards,
your business cards, your mortgage
and frequent-flyer miles keep you
at a charitable distance.

But, he is too deliberate and pays
no attention as you pass by to pay
full price for goods no lips
have touched. How does he

not care you see him like this,
indulging in intimate waste
like a child who knows no better
or a man whose shame
rinses off in public showers?

Is this the life Thoreau wanted driven
into a corner to "suck out
all the marrow," and "reduce it
to its lowest terms"? Maybe this man

has that and maybe in that corner
something rich drums his bones
when he warms his hands around
the fifty-gallon barrel of fire
his three best friends keep burning.

You want to say "Good God, man,"
but you keep your comments
to yourself and on your way out
inhale his smoke like a spirit

you might someday need to call
to life.

WHO, YOU?

The darker you, darker
than Jungian shadow,
the other side of Other,

the you so distant
if someone demanded
"Who do you think you are?"

you'd be deep-sea-adrift,
some creature's shape
rising hard below you.

Aberrant, kinky, bad seed:
no use to name it, DSM-V
won't discuss it.

It's the you who rolls
your lover over at 3 a.m.
and commands positions,

it's the you desperate to love,
desperate to let yourself
be loved but able only

to roll your lover over at 3 a.m.
and command positions
you might never get out of.

SENDING ANNA HOME

They are sending Anna home,
scrubbed and sterile,
void of superstition.

They slid white gloves
up and down the hallways
in her mind,

pried open doors,
kicked out windows,
found nothing.

She had one final bluster,
before they strapped her down
and plugged her in:

"Rescue on the way," he said,
then burned to the ground
an architecture

twenty-six years in the making.
She stares out the window
at the birds flying south,

who look down
but never back:
an omen that once

had meaning, but now
she can't be sure
since every thought needs

to be thought twice.

OUTSIDE THE FACT

There is a window
in Sandra's mind
framed by walls of fire
where chiffon curtains
never burn,
as if they hung
outside the fact
of fire.

There are no clear views,
little more
than vague shapes floating,
which try to enter
by way of fire but perish
in crossing.

Down a narrow hallway
in a dark room,
a clouded window hides
a screen that is breathing,
filled with rainwater.

The wind keeps aloft
a scrambling of words
and feeds the fire.

She writes her name in ash
along the sill.

ALL GROWN UP

Each evening she watched,
but the door never opened.
Voices grew faint.

She stayed in the corner,
stared out at the moon.
The moon stared back.

Pages in her open songbook
fluttered like birds
frightened into flight.

The parched tongue
of some lost wind
carried her song away.

The room grew half,
then quarter, dividing
its way down to surround

one shard of moonlight,
constant in the corner.
The world outside grew large,

and what was there to do
but leave herself behind,

watching shadows break the light
beneath her door.

DIVINER

She sings in choir
to lose herself
in unison.

She turns on lights
in the room before
the one she enters
to enter shadow first.

She drops her chin
and speaks
toward her heart,
then looks at me
askant.

She writes letters
to people she loves
and keeps them
unsigned
in a drawer beside
her bed.

She believes a world
she believed long ago
will still come true
if she figures out
the color scheme
of her living room.

She is like a seed
that stays dormant
season after season,
certain the light
next year will find her
deeper than light
has ever gone.

HER SONG

is an urge to swim at night
past the breaking sea,

the underside of an eyelid
quivering on dream,

the fist against one's gut
dead lost in the twilit wild,

perfumed décolletage
of a beautiful woman

who leaves the party early
and alone.

IV.

FOR THE WALGREENS CHRISTMAS EVE CREW

I have cursed you and will do so again
for sticking price tags over directions
on my poison ivy lotion, for misshelving
the buy-one-get-one free 64 oz. Gatorade.
I have cursed your polyester vests that fit
like grocery bags folded too many times,
your crooked name tags, your programmed
statements of appreciation for my business.

But, tonight I bless you. It's Christmas Eve,
and no place else is open, open and brightly
inviting for those of us without companions.
My wife walked out two weeks ago, and I cannot
bring myself to finish the tree with tinsel.
It comforts me to know you, too, are stuck
inside fluorescent haze and hum,
while those you love go on without you.

I have come to buy three wax logs
because I need to build a fire, a hearth,
something warm to tend. I stand
too long in the aisle marked *Seasonal,*
hoping my mood will pass.

The night janitor approaches, catches
my heel with his mop. "I'm sorry, sir,"
he mutters, but before he can finish, I say,
"No, forgive me, please, forgive me,"
and in that extra plea I hear the voice
of a man on his knees begging too long,

too loud, a man on his knees lost
in prayer to false gods when small talk
at the dinner table might have saved him,
a man on his knees unable to rise
from beside the plastic crèche
on sale for 7.95.

BLUE TIME

"Ruthie died 15 minutes ahead of Verena," Mrs. Cady said. "Verena talked about the whole thing. She said, 'This is the time we're going to be dying.'

"She said to go get Daddy, and she gave me a list of friends she wanted to give flowers to. She asked to be cremated because she didn't want to be in a box, she wanted to be free."

Ruthie and Verena Cady
Siamese Twins, 1984–1991

The three-chambered heart you share
beats now for one. Your sister is gone
beside you. Her eyes are glazed,
rolled up as if she were in rapture
between two notes, legato diminuendo.
Your eyes, too, grow dim,
like stones sinking in deep,
clear water.

In the fading light, a warm hand
from a blue time behind
cups the nape of your neck
and guides you to a meadow
where two souls embrace,
each one free, each one.

BE QUIET

I.

If no one listens,
work the silence.

Multiply one
by less

for the friction
of fraction; heat

has heart, as bloodless
as diamond, dense

and faceted, many-
faced, blank-faced,

facing
a blank wall; echo

is stone heard hard.

II.

I knew a man
whose hands

were all he held
of this world,

and when
he folded his palms

in prayer
like wings,

they were god
enough

and moist
like the tongue

of some holy,
holy spirit,

sitting silent.

IF YOU HAD TO

I visited Ellen's tomb and opened the coffin.
—RALPH WALDO EMERSON,
JOURNAL ENTRY FOR MARCH 29, 1832

If you had to see,
had to unearth and open
a loved one's casket,
not for closure
but for the wound

more alive than you
might ever be again,
the wound whose flesh
ripened like fruit
brought to table,

you would see love
has no memory, love
is a field
whose distance grows
the deeper in you go.

You would see
someone you love
is nothing but time
spun through space
into which you lean

to keep yourself longer
than memory can recall.
Let's just say, you had to live
because you were all
love had.

EVEN THE DISHES

Alone tonight at dinner,
I felt the plate go flat,
the wine glass crack

as if we all opened
to the end when wind
rushes in and letters

unhinge from our names.
The glass held my hand
as much as I held it,

as if we pressed each other
to keep round this world.
"I-thou" the wine glass said

and looked right through me.
When you live this long alone,
objects draw close to fill space

gesture and touch flesh out,
memories burn and prick
like stars in Doppler retreat

below your skin.
"Love me," your bones intone
around a fire that you tend, rapt

to hear stories of others
who live alone and bother to say
"even the dishes"

as if to affirm like family
or some such heat that warms
where you must have lived.

BELOW THE GOSPEL TENT

—Kansas City Jazz and Blues Festival 1999

In gold lamé suits, white shirts,
and black ties, the Crown Seekers
give it up and give it up again
to their souls' sweet surrender.
They are lost in the music's pulse,
the falsetto howl of pure joy.
I have not known such rapture
since Donna Summer thumpa-thumpa-
thumped me into a disco fever.
Who cares the color of our skin?
Who cares the gangly arcs my arms
traject, here, at God's doorstep.
We are into each other's skin,
sharing the heat and humidity
hovering like salvation in this tent.
Our raised arms wave and keep the beat.
The Crown Seekers mop each other's brow.
We are rhapsodic psychotic, delirious
to the point of holy confession.
Chucka-chucka-chucka goes the guitar.
Whoops and howls fly to Jesus Christ on high.
He is there. He is here. Angels simmer
beneath the drummer's hi-hat cymbals.
The bass player's whumpa-whumpa whacks my groin.
We just dropped in for the good vibes, and now,
we are the good vibes, one holy rolling mass
pointing skyward to a point out of sight.
We are ready to give it up, give *it* up!
But, listen. Three hundred yards away

on the blues stage, someone's heart
is breaking, someone is down too low
to crawl, too heavy to go on.
And now, someone leans hard on the B string,
bending at the twenty-first fret until it sounds
like he has screamed his belly wide open.
My buddy and I mop our own brows
with our own bandanas. If we give it up now,
what good is there to feel the pain? Pain
is what keeps us moving toward each other.
How long can the rapture sustain?
We can get high on highs,
or we can get high on lows.
We rise to leave, to get down
and stick close to what we know
with our lawn chairs and cold beer.

BELIEVERS

Chased by fire up an Idaho hillside,
one man paused, struck a match
and burned a path to freedom.
He believed in fire, the others
in themselves, and so they burned
to ash.

Capsized, two men swam hard
for shore. One of them saw light
behind and turned back out to sea.
He clung all night to the buoy
and was rescued early morning
by the boat that found, close
to shore, his dead companion.

Inside what he believed a bottomless
crevasse, a climber cut his rope and fell
to darkness that filled each hour with light
toward an exit. He lived to climb,
but he knew life tends downward
and was delivered.

About to be raped, a woman yelled "Fire,"
and help arrived. She knew "Help"
doesn't draw like "Fire."
Sometimes you have to threaten
someone's life to save your own.

New Testament Church down the street
wants my neighbor to give himself over
so the Lord can shake his alcoholic demons.
My neighbor says "Satan sits down and drinks
with me, but Jesus only preaches."

He takes one drink each day to prove
the demon has no power, and while he sips
his bourbon at the corner bar, he reads
the New Testament aloud to drunks
who believe they're damned but burn
to know why.

LAST RITES

Just before you die, you recall
making love to your wife
one cold night in a mountain cabin,
the fireplace
sibilant with coals.

You lay in silence,
your finger tapping a meter
up the small of her back.
You wanted to sing, to string
a simple tune up her spine
and trill across her shoulders.

You drifted, instead, to sleep,
both arms around her,
and before you fell under,
as if she heard your song,
she brought your hand to her lips,

and you knew for certain
she had saved all her life
to buy your way into this world,
this one warm
in the palm of your hand.

IN QUIET CAFES

—For Edward Hopper

Late afternoon
in quiet cafes, the dead
sit down and rest.

They spirit in shadow,
sip tea tepid and weak,
no sugar, no cream.

They test the waters
of this world to ease
back in. Stare, and

they will stare
but to one side.
They believe

you believe
their spirit lives
in your belief.

Sit with them
alone, they
who come this far,

this weary
and sit in public rooms
open to you

who long to hold them
but will not go so far
as to pass the sugar

pouring sweetly now
into your tea, hot,
"Good God," you say,

"too hot to drink."

STREWN

What brings you David Zimmerman to mind?
It is dusk, St. Louis January, and Sunday.
I am bicycling on the river trail.
The darker night falls
the faster I go because something
is after me.

I spent another weekend alone.
It is cold, and tears stream off my chin
as if I am able to cry,
but I cannot tell if the cold stings
or helps me weep
because I cannot help myself. I am tired
of another night seeping deep
without someone to call me home.

When you were struck by a car,
hitchhiking home on Christmas Eve
with toy dishes for your little sister
and had your leg cut off
later that night, such pain
did not know my world.

I was seven and you fifteen.
I believed the nimbus of baby Jesus,
Santa's watchful eye, the bounty in
Montgomery Ward's Christmas catalog
if I was good.

You come to me now in one
of those images unbidden,
lodged in some vital organ
soon to give up.

Strewn across two lanes,
were blood-spattered dishes,
you on your gravel-scoured back,
staring into the Milky Way,
sirens in the silent night.

Every night is Christmas Eve, David, starry
and silent on its gravel-scoured back. I pray
you are these many years gone well and able
to still imagine your sister's joy tomorrow.

SWEET ASSASSIN

> *She would of been a good woman if it had been somebody there to shoot her every day of her life.*
> —The Misfit in Flannery O'Connor's
>   "A Good Man is Hard to Find"

The barrel of his gun rimmed a crescent
in my forehead and quickened me

as poignant as a man struck blind
high speed on an icy road.

Knives inside my throat ignited,
and every breath swelled orchestral.

There I was, alive and able in a whisper
to calm the trigger of this young man,

so scared and angry he saw himself in me
and said how far he would go, but then

he couldn't and cursed me in flight.
Come back, my sweet assassin, you

who returned all my words to flesh.
I never believed I was enough to die for,

until you, dear life, looked me in the eye
and said "Don't think I won't, motherfucker,"

and I knew you would
if I did not stare you down,

and take you back, back below my flesh,
flushed right then with blood my body swore

like an oath I must repeat high speed
on an icy road to nowhere that would have me.

FINAL DRAFT OF A NOTE TO MYSELF

Find some acreage
where broken plows rust to soil,
where fence posts lean as if boundaries gave up,
where the fence is barbed but now for what?

What you keep this side is yours,
heartbeat and pulse, footstep
and grip, private fires you choose
to contain.

Everyone you loved has gone.
You will never be happy
the way you could have been,
the way happiness insists.

Let the creek, ridge, and fallen tree
suggest where the dog should stay,
the dog whose name you change
each day, the dog

who wanders in one day like a fetish.
Make for him a home, and
a temple shall rise around you.

Sit down on a front porch
that faces no road
or any way out
you know of. Limit

what lawfully you call yours.
Be happy when it feels.

ACKNOWLEDGEMENTS

The author gratefully acknowledges the following publications, in which some of the poems herein originally appeared:

Cape Rock: "Sending Anna Home"

Defined Providence: "Still Moving"

Cimarron Review: "Had Anyone Cared to Listen"

Natural Bridge: "Love Would be Good"; "All Grown Up"; "Come Shivering to Collect"

Margie: "At the Back of His Cage"

Evansville Review: "Stray"

Connecticut Review: "Brother, Can You?"

Atlanta Review: "For the Walgreens Christmas Eve Crew"

Green Hills Literary Lantern: "Falsetto"

Antioch Review: "Syllabic"

Gettysburg Review: "Head On"; "Look Twice Before Crossing"

Poetry Daily: "Look Twice Before Crossing"

2nd & Church: "In Quiet Cafes"

The Penn Review: "Taxonomy"

With deep gratitude to Howard Schwartz, Professor Emeritus University of Missouri-St. Louis, for his early encouragement of my work and his continuing mentorship.

This book was set in ITC Galliard, designed by Matthew Carter and published in 1978. It is based on the sixteenth-century type created by Robert Granjon. The name Galliard refers to a lively dance of that era and Carter's type has long been admired for both its energy and elegance. It is perhaps best known for its "pelican-beak" italic letter "*g*."

This book was designed by Shannon Carter, Ian Creeger, and Gregory Wolfe. It was published in hardcover, paperback, and electronic formats by Slant Books, Seattle, Washington.

www.ingramcontent.com/pod-product-compliance
Lightning Source LLC
Chambersburg PA
CBHW051658040426
42446CB00009B/1201